Everything I've Learned

100 Great Principles to Live By

Edited by Leslie Pockell
with Adrienne Avila

WARNER BOOKS

New York   Boston

Warner Books

Time Warner Book Group
1271 Avenue of the Americas, New York, NY 10020
Visit our Web site at www.twbookmark.com

Printed in the United States of America
First Printing: May 2004
10 9 8 7 6 5 4 3 2 1

ISBN : 0-446-52345-3
LCCN : 2004101219

Book design and composition by Mada Design, Inc.

It is a good thing
for an uneducated man
to read books of quotations.

- Winston Churchill

INTRODUCTION

For whatever reason, we seem to be living at a time when established institutions are failing to provide both moral instruction and the sort of practical advice that might prepare individuals of any age to confront the uncertainties of life. Accordingly, our objective in compiling this book of principles is to supply readers with an essential arsenal of wisdom gathered from the insights and observations of those who have learned from experience what life is all about. The sources are as ancient as the Delphic Oracle and as contemporary as Mother Teresa and Woody Allen. The wise men and women represented here are soldiers and pacifists, poets, politicians, and philosophers. The principles themselves are in the form of aphorisms, poems, and prayers; from Jewish, Christian, Muslim, Buddhist, and secular traditions. Some of them relate to a sense of self-worth, while others are directed outward. Some are concerned with spiritual awareness, and others with success in practical matters. Sometimes humorous, sometimes sobering, sometimes inspiring, these are words of wisdom that we have found to be illuminating and helpful.

For those moments of uncertainty and doubt we all face, when we're looking for encouragement or advice and don't know where to turn, keep this book nearby. Somewhere in its contents we're sure you'll find the words you need to guide you on your way.

Leslie Pockell
Adrienne Avila

CONTENTS

PART I

Be True to Yourself

Know thyself.

- Inscription at the Delphic Oracle

Keep true to the dreams of your youth.

- Friedrich von Schiller

Following your heart's desire will lead you
in the direction your spirit wants to go.

- *Oprah Winfrey*

A musician must make music,
an artist must paint, a poet must write,
if he is to be ultimately at peace with himself.
What a man can be, he must be.

- *Abraham Maslow*

This above all: to thine own self be true,
And it must follow, as the night the day,
Thou canst not then be false to any man.

- *William Shakespeare,* Hamlet

No man can wear one face to himself and another to the multitude without finally getting bewildered as to which may be true.

- *Nathaniel Hawthorne*

Know then thyself, presume not God to scan;
The proper study of mankind is Man.

- Alexander Pope

Noght o word spak he moore than was neede,
And that was seyd in forme and reverence,
And short and quyk, and ful of hy sentence;
Sowynge in moral vertu was his speche,
And gladly wolde he lerne, and gladly teche.

Not one word spoke he more than was his need;
And that was said in fullest reverence
And short and quick and full of high good sense.
Pregnant of moral virtue was his speech;
And gladly would he learn and gladly teach.

*- Geoffrey Chaucer, describing the scholar in the
"General Prologue" to* The Canterbury Tales

You don't ever have to do anything sensational
to love or to be loved.

- *Fred Rogers*

Have nothing in your houses
that you do not know to be useful
or believe to be beautiful.

- *William Morris*

You must have a room, or a certain hour or so a day, where you don't know what was in the newspaper that morning . . . a place where you can simply experience and bring forth what you are and what you might be.

- *Joseph Campbell*

PART II

Be Mindful of Others

Do to others as thou wouldst they should do to thee, and
Do to none other but as thou wouldst be done to.

*- First printed version of the Golden Rule in English,
attributed to Socrates by Richard Woodville,
Earl Rivers, in* Dictes and Sayengis of the Philosophres, *1477*

He could have added fortune to fame, but caring for neither, he found happiness in being helpful to the world.

- *Epitaph on the grave of George Washington Carver*

He that plants trees loves others beside himself.

- Thomas Fuller

The greatest pleasure I know
is to do a good action by stealth,
and to have it found out by accident.

- *Charles Lamb*

Love your neighbor, but don't pull down the hedge.

- *Swiss proverb*

And what does the LORD require of you?
To act justly and to love mercy
and to walk humbly with your God.

- Micah 6:8

PART III

Be Direct and Confident

Do, or do not. There is no "try."

- *Yoda in* The Empire Strikes Back

Do not wait for leaders; do it alone, person to person.

- *Mother Teresa*

You are a king by your own fireside,
as much as any monarch on his throne.

- *Miguel de Cervantes*

Cautious, careful people, always casting about to preserve their reputation and social standing, never can bring about a reform. Those who are really in earnest must be willing to be anything or nothing in the world's estimation.

- Susan B. Anthony

Be not the first by whom the new is tried,
Nor yet the last to lay the old aside.

- Anonymous, quoted by Dwight D. Eisenhower

I believe life is a series of near misses.
A lot of what we ascribe to luck is not luck at all.
It's seizing the day and accepting responsibility
for your future. It's seeing what other people don't see
and pursuing that vision.

- Lewis Grizzard

A man who is being delivered from the danger of a fierce lion does not object, whether this service is performed by an unknown or an illustrious individual. Why, therefore, do people seek knowledge from celebrities?

- Sufi mystic El Ghazali

Don't think of retiring from the world
until the world will be sorry that you retire.
I hate a fellow whom pride or cowardice or laziness
drives into a corner, and who does nothing when he is there
but sit and growl. Let him come out as I do, and bark.

- Samuel Johnson

Count that day lost whose low descending sun
views from thy hand no worthy action done.

- *Anonymous*

To live—do you know what that means?
To undo your belt and look for trouble!

- *Nikos Kazantzakis,* Zorba the Greek

The safest course is to do nothing against one's conscience. With this secret, we can enjoy life and have no fear of death.

- Voltaire

He who has nothing to die for has nothing to live for.

- Moroccan proverb

Life is painting a picture, not doing a sum.

- *Oliver Wendell Holmes, Jr.*

I never submitted the whole system of my opinions to the creed of any party of men whatever, in religion, in philosophy, in politics or anything else, where I was capable of thinking for myself. Such an addiction is the last degradation of a free and moral agent. If I could go to Heaven but with a party, I would not go there at all.

- Thomas Jefferson

PART IV

Be Prudent and Practical

If you tell the truth, you don't have to remember anything.

- *Mark Twain*

There's a sucker born every minute, and two to take him.

- *Attributed to P. T. Barnum*

You can't cheat an honest man.

- *W. C. Fields*

You can keep your mouth closed
and run the risk that people will think you are a fool,
or open it and remove all doubt.

- Anonymous

No one can make you feel inferior without your consent.

- Eleanor Roosevelt

Annual income twenty pounds,
annual expenditure nineteen nineteen six, result happiness.
Annual income twenty pounds, annual expenditure
twenty pounds ought and six, result misery.

- *Charles Dickens,* David Copperfield

If you lend someone twenty dollars,
and never see that person again, it was
probably worth the money.

- Anonymous

The quickest way to double your money
is to fold it in half and put it back in your pocket.

- *Anonymous*

Money will buy a bed, but not sleep;
Books, but not brains;
Food, but not appetite;
Finery, but not beauty;
A house, but not a home;
Medicine, but not health;
Luxuries, but not culture;
Amusement, but not happiness;
Religion, but not salvation;
A passport to everywhere but heaven.

- Anonymous

Never play poker with a man called Pop.
Never eat at a place called Mom's.

- Anonymous

Never test the depth of the water with both feet.

- *Anonymous*

Never apologize, it's a sign of weakness.

- John Wayne

Always do sober what you said you'd do drunk. That will teach you to keep your mouth shut.

- Ernest Hemingway

He who hesitates is a damned fool!

- *Mae West*

No bastard ever won a war by dying
for his country. You win the war by making
the other poor dumb bastard die for his country!

- *General George S. Patton, Jr.*

A man's feet should be planted in his country, but his eyes should survey the world.

- *George Santayana*

PART V

Be Accommodating
(Life Is Unpredictable)

My momma always said,
"Life is like a box of chocolates.
You never know what you're gonna get."

- *Forrest Gump, in* Forrest Gump, *by Winston Groom*

Life is so largely controlled by chance
that its conduct can be but a perpetual improvisation.

- W. Somerset Maugham

Life consists not in holding good cards
but in playing well those you hold.

- *Josh Billings*

All the art of living lies in a fine mingling of letting go and holding on.

- Havelock Ellis

The art of living is more like that of wrestling than dancing. The main thing is to stand firm and be ready for an unseen attack.

- *Marcus Aurelius,* Meditations

A foolish consistency is the hobgoblin of little minds, adored by little statesmen and philosophers and divines.

- Ralph Waldo Emerson

PART VI

Be Flexible
(Life Is Not Fair)

In three words I can sum up
everything I've learned about life: it goes on.

- Robert Frost

There are those who argue that everything breaks even in this old dump of a world of ours. I suppose the ginks who argue that way hold that, because the rich man gets ice in the summer and the poor man gets it in the winter, things are breaking even for both. Maybe so, but I'll swear I can't see it that way.

- Bat Masterson

There is always inequity in life. Some men
are killed in a war and some men are wounded,
and some men never leave the country. . . . Life is unfair.

- *John F. Kennedy*

Let me not pray to be sheltered from dangers
but to be fearless in facing them.
Let me not beg for the stilling of my pain
but for the heart to conquer it.
Let me not look to allies in life's battlefield
but to my own strengths.
Let me not crave in anxious fear to be saved
but hope for the patience to win my freedom.

-Prayer of the Bodhisattva

The *paramitas* are six stages of study and practice followed by the Bodhisattvas in their progress to Buddhahood. They are (1) charity, or alms-giving; (2) discipline, or observance of precepts; (3) forbearance, or patient resignation; (4) energy; (5) concentration; and (6) wisdom.

The Serenity Prayer

God, give us grace to accept with serenity
the things that cannot be changed,
courage to change the things
which should be changed, and the wisdom
to distinguish the one from the other.

- Reinhold Niebuhr

If

If you can keep your head when all about you
  Are losing theirs and blaming it on you;
If you can trust yourself when all men doubt you,
  But make allowance for their doubting too;
If you can wait and not be tired by waiting,
  Or being lied about, don't deal in lies,
Or being hated don't give way to hating,
  And yet don't look too good, nor talk too wise;

If you can dream—and not make dreams your master;
If you can think—and not make thoughts your aim;
  If you can meet with triumph and disaster
  And treat those two impostors just the same;
If you can bear to hear the truth you've spoken
  Twisted by knaves to make a trap for fools,
Or watch the things you gave your life to, broken,
  And stoop and build 'em up with worn-out tools;

If you can make one heap of all your winnings
And risk it on one turn of pitch-and-toss,
And lose, and start again at your beginnings
And never breathe a word about your loss;
If you can force your heart and nerve and sinew
To serve your turn long after they are gone,
And so hold on when there is nothing in you
Except the Will which says to them: "Hold on";

If you can talk with crowds and keep your virtue,
Or walk with Kings—nor lose the common touch;
If neither foes nor loving friends can hurt you;
If all men count with you, but none too much;
If you can fill the unforgiving minute
With sixty seconds' worth of distance run,
Yours is the Earth and everything that's in it,
And—which is more—you'll be a Man, my son.

-Rudyard Kipling

The Last Freedom

We who lived in concentration camps can remember the men who walked through the huts comforting others, giving away their last piece of bread. They may have been few in number, but they offer sufficient proof that everything can be taken from a man but one thing: the last of the human freedoms— to choose one's attitude in any given set of circumstances, to choose one's own way.

- *Viktor E. Frankl*

Who Counts

It is not the critic who counts, nor the man who points out how the strong man stumbles, or where the doer of deeds could have done better. The credit belongs to the man who is actually in the arena; whose face is marred by dust and sweat; who strives valiantly; who errs and may fail again, because there is no effort without error or shortcoming, but who does actually strive to do the deeds; who does know the great enthusiasm, the great devotion; who spends himself in a worthy cause; who at best, knows in the end the triumph of high achievement, and who at worst, if he fails, at least fails while daring greatly, so that his place shall never be with those cold and timid souls who know neither victory nor defeat.

- *Theodore Roosevelt*

An ancient said,
"When confusion ceases,
tranquility comes;
when tranquility comes,
wisdom appears,
and when wisdom appears,
reality is seen."

- Keizan Jokan

Who will tell whether one happy moment
of love or the joy of breathing or walking
on a bright morning and smelling the fresh air,
is not worth all the suffering
and effort which life implies?

- *Erich Fromm*

The happiness of life is made up of
minute fractions—the little
soon forgotten charities of a kiss
or smile, a kind look,
a heartfelt compliment.

- *Samuel Taylor Coleridge*

And we should consider every day lost
on which we have not danced at least once.
And we should call every truth false
which was not accompanied by at least one laugh.

- *Friedrich Nietzsche*

Just living is not enough. One must have sunshine, freedom, and a little flower.

- *Hans Christian Andersen*

We can't all be heroes because someone has to sit on the curb and clap as they go by.

- Will Rogers

Fiat justicia, ruat coelum.

(Let justice be done, though the heavens fall.)

- Latin maxim, attributed to
Lucius Calpurnius Piso Caesoninus

Believe that life is worth living
and your belief will help create the fact.

- *William James*

PART VII

Be Aware of Today

You will never be happy if you continue to search for what happiness consists of. You will never live if you are looking for the meaning of life.

- *Albert Camus*

You're only here for a short visit.
Don't hurry. Don't worry.
And be sure to smell the flowers
along the way.

- Walter C. Hagen

My advice to you is not to inquire why or whither, but just enjoy your ice cream while it's on your plate — that's my philosophy.

- *Thornton Wilder,* The Skin of Our Teeth

I have a simple philosophy:
    Fill what's empty.
    Empty what's full.
    Scratch where it itches.

- Alice Roosevelt Longworth

There is only one success—
to be able to spend your life in your own way.

- Christopher Morley

Live as if you were to die tomorrow. Learn as if you were to live forever.

- *Mahatma Gandhi*

If you're not failing every now and again,
it's a sign you are playing it safe.

- *Woody Allen*

You don't get to choose how you're going to die, or when.
You can only decide how you're going to live, now.

- Joan Baez

Wherever your life ends, it is all there.
The advantage of living is not measured by length,
but by use; some men have lived long, and lived little;
attend to it while you are in it. It lies in your will,
not in the number of years, for you to have lived enough.

- *Michel de Montaigne*

Life has meaning only if one barters it day by day
for something other than itself.

- *Antoine de Saint-Exupéry*

If you're alive you've got to flap your arms
and legs, you've got to jump around a lot,
for life is the very opposite of death,
and therefore you must at the very least
think noisily and colorfully, or you're not alive.

- Mel Brooks

When I stand before God at the end of my life,
I would hope that I would not have a single bit of talent left,
and could say, "I used everything you gave me."

- *Erma Bombeck*

PART VIII

Be Humble
and Love All Good Things

Love many things, for therein lies the true strength,
and whoever loves much, performs much,
and can accomplish much,
and that which is done in love is well done.

- Vincent van Gogh

Some people think only intellect counts:
knowing how to solve problems, knowing how to
get by, knowing how to identify an advantage and seize it.
But the functions of intellect are insufficient without
courage, love, friendship, compassion, and empathy.

- *Dean Koontz*

There is time for work. And time for love.
That leaves no other time.

- Coco Chanel

Fear less, hope more;
whine less, breathe more;
talk less, say more;
hate less, love more;
and all good things are yours.

- Swedish proverb

To be without some of the things you want
is an indispensable part of happiness.

- *Bertrand Russell*

This is what you shall do: Love the earth and sun and animals, despise riches, give alms to everyone that asks, stand up for the stupid and crazy, devote your income and labor to others, hate tyrants, argue not concerning God, have patience and indulgence toward the people, take off your hat to nothing known or unknown or to any man or number of men, go freely with powerful uneducated persons and with the young and with the mothers of families, read these leaves in the open air every season of every year of your life, re-examine all you have been told at school or church or in any book, dismiss whatever insults your own soul, and your very flesh shall be a great poem and have the richest fluency not only in its words but in the silent lines of its lips and face and between lashes of your eyes and in every motion and joint of your body . . .

- Walt Whitman

First do no harm.

- Hippocrates

Other Books Edited by Leslie Pockell

The 100 Best Poems of All Time
The 100 Best Love Poems of All Time
The 13 Best Horror Stories of All Time